✣ POEM OF THE DEEP SONG

POEM OF THE DEEP SONG

POEMA DEL CANTE JONDO

by

Federico García Lorca

Translated by
Carlos Bauer

City Lights Books
San Francisco

©1931, 1987 by City Lights Books
Translation ©1987 by Carlos Bauer
All Rights Reserved

Poema del cante jondo was first published by Ulises: Madrid, 1931.

Cover design by Gent Sturgeon

Library of Congress Cataloging-in-Publication Data
García Lorca, Federico, 1898-1936
  Poem of the deep song.
  Translation of: Poema del cante jondo.
  I. Title
PQ6613.A763P613   1987   861'.62   87-11806
ISBN: 0-87286-204-6
ISBN: 0-87286-205-4 (pbk)

City Lights Books are available to bookstores through our primary
distributor: Subterranean Company. P. O. Box 168, 265 S. 5th St.,
Monroe, OR 97456. 503-847-5274. Toll-free orders 800-274-7826.
FAX 503-847-6018. Our books are also available through library
jobbers and regional distributors. For personal orders and catalogs,
please write to City Lights Books, 261 Columbus Avenue, San
Francisco CA 94133.

CITY LIGHTS BOOKS are edited by Lawrence Ferlinghetti and
Nancy J. Peters and published at the City Lights Bookstore, 261
Columbus Avenue, San Francisco, CA 94133.

CONTENTS

Introduction by Carlos Bauer   i

Baladilla de los Tres Ríos / Little Ballad of the Three Rivers   2

POEMA DE LA SIGUIRIYA GITANA

Paisaje / Landscape   6
La Guitarra / The Guitar   8
El Grito / The Cry   10
El Silencio / The Silence   12
El Paso de la Siguiriya / The Passing Stage of the *Siguiriya*   14
Después de Pasar / After Passing By   16
Y Después / And After That   18

POEMA DE LA SOLEÁ

Evocación / Evocation   20
Pueblo / Village   22
Puñal / Dagger   24
Encrucijada / Crossroads   26
¡Ay! / Ay!   28
Sorpresa / Surprise   30
La Soleá / The *Soleá*   32
Cueva / Cave   34
Encuentro / Encounter   36
Alba / Dawn   38

POEMA DE LA SAETA

Arqueros / Archers   40
Noche / Night   42
Sevilla / Sevilla   44
Procesión / Procession   46
Paso / Stage   48
Saeta / Saeta   50
Balcón / Balcony   52
Madrugada / Before the Dawn   54

GRÁFICO DE LA PETENERA

Campaña / Bell 56
Camino / Road 58
Las Seis Cuerdas / The Six Strings 60
Danza / Dance 62
Muerte de la Petenera / Death of the Petenera 64
Falseta / Guitar Flourish 66
De Profundis / De Profundis 68
Clamor / Death Knell 70

DOS MUCHACHAS

La Lola / Lola 72
Amparo / Amparo 74

VIÑETAS FLAMENCAS

Retrato de Silverio Franconetti / Portrait of
   Silverio Franconetti 76
Juan Breva / Juan Breva 78
Café Cantante / Flamenco Cabaret 80
Lamentación de la Muerte / Lamentation of Death 82
Conjuro / Incantation 84
Memento / Memento 86

TRES CIUDADES

Malagueña / Malagueña 88
Barrio de Córdoba / Neighborhood in Cordoba 90
Baile / Dance 92

SEIS CAPRICHOS

Adivinanza de la Guitarra / Riddle of the Guitar 94
Candil / Oil Lamp 96
Crótalo / Castanet 98
Chumbera / Prickly Pear 100
Pita / Maguey Plant 102
Cruz / Cross 104

ESCENA DEL TENIENTE CORONEL
DE LA GUARDIA CIVIL

Cuarto de Banderas / Guardroom   106

Canción del Gitano Apaleado / Song of the Beaten Gypsy   114

DIÁLOGO DEL AMARGO

Campo / Countryside   116

Canción de la Madre del Amargo / Song of Amargo's Mother   131

Translator's Notes   133

INTRODUCTION

In 1921, Federico García Lorca wrote his first major work, *Poem of the Deep Song*. With this short book of poems, the twenty-three-year old poet had crystallized the themes that would run through all his great works: love, death, and alienation. For Lorca, this book represents a first step of exploration into the existential character of the Andalusian soul. Lorca employed the same outlet — though in a somewhat different way — that the Andalusian people had traditionally used to express their feelings: deep song.

A few words about deep song or *cante jondo*. Lorca's own ideas about its origins were influenced by the research of his friend, the composer Manuel de Falla. Lorca: "The historical events Falla [says] have influenced [our] songs are three: the Spanish Church adopting the Byzantine liturgical chant, the Saracen invasion, the arrival of numerous bands of Gypsies. They are those mysterious, wandering folk who gave deep song its definitive form." Ten years later, after new studies had been published in Spain, Lorca would speak of the Sephardic influence on deep song. Most students of Spanish folk music believe that an antecedent to deep song — combining native Andalusian, Arab and Hebrew elements — existed prior to the arrival of the Gypsies from India in 1477. What they maintain is that each succeeding immigration — especially Jew, Moor and Gypsy — grafted onto the primitive Andalusian folk song parts of their own musical traditions.

Critics hold flamenco in lesser esteem than deep song, viewing flamenco as a mere shadow of deep song, which has a far greater emotional and lyric impact. (An analagous situation in American music might be the relationship between blues and rock and roll.) Or as Lorca himself put it: "Local color [flamenco] as opposed to spiritual color [deep song] — that is the profound difference."

Cante jondo, in the 1880s, went from the seedy tavern to the cabaret and, in the process, changed from the plaintive, solitary cry of the Andalusian soul into the musical hall spectacular of flamenco, where flashy commercialism gradually prevailed.

Lorca presents the four major songs that comprise *cante jondo*:

The Gypsy Siguiriya. Lorca believed this song to be the "genuine, perfect prototype" of deep song, the one that most preserved its ancient oriental origins. *Siguiriyas* are sung with a rising emotional tension, interrupted by sudden cries of anguish (the *ay!*), and unexpected silences. The song ends with a gradual fading away of both voice and guitar. The lyrics express life's most tragic dramas, its intensest moments. Because of its extreme emotional demands, mastering the *siguiriya* is the apex of a singer's quest.

The Soleá. Soleá is an Andalusian corruption of *soledad*, solitude. This song looks back to a tragic past. The mood is melancholy, and the lyrics show a resignation to fate. The *soleá* is also intended for dance.

The Saeta. This song is a musical prayer that is sung during Holy Week in Sevilla. It is always sung without guitar accompaniment, and always sung to Christ or the Virgin, representations of whom are carried through the streets on hand-held floats (the Stages of the Passion). When the procession stops, a *saeta* is sung as an offering. *Saeta* means arrow or barb, and Lorca plays on its double meaning; the piercing cries of the *saeta* become arrows, and the singers of *saetas* become archers.

The Petenera. The *petenera* is not usually considered to be part of *cante jondo* but rather an intermediate song, halfway between *cante jondo* and flamenco. Derived from Andalusian folk song, it was later given its final form by Sephardic Jews. It is intended for dance, and has guitar accompaniment. Its themes resemble those of the *soleá*, as does its mood of bitter fatalism.

For years it had been assumed that Lorca wrote *Poem of the Deep Song* specifically for the "Competition of Deep Song," which was organized by Lorca and Manuel de Falla, and held in Granada during June of 1922. Recent scholarship, however, has shown that the seeds — if not the actual writing of this book — were germinating long before the idea of a competition had even been suggested. The group to which García Lorca and Falla belonged were concerned that deep song would disappear, as were many other Spaniards. (Lorca would later say: "The artistic treasure of an entire race is on the road to oblivion...Old men are taking to the grave priceless treasures of past generations. . . .") Although the group had originally wanted to start a *café cantante* dedicated to the preservation of deep song, the project was never realized; but near the end of 1921 the idea of the competition began to take shape. More than likely, Lorca began writing parts of "Poem of the *Saeta*" not long after a Holy Week excursion to Sevilla he made with Falla in the spring of 1921, that had affected him profoundly.

Poem of the Deep Song was first published in 1931, a decade after it was written; however, it is not far different from the 1921 manuscript. In readying the work for publication, Lorca restructured the end of the book, made some final corrections, and added two dramatic dialogues (written in 1925) to fill out a very short volume of poems. He also eliminated some fourteen poems from the book, though some had already been crossed out in pencil in the original manuscript.

Poem of the Deep Song is in no way a book of imitation *cante jondo* lyrics, rather it is an exploration into the soul of this Gypsy-Andalusian-flamenco cosmos: the poems are images provoked by deep song, the emotions produced within the listener. Yet while Lorca strove to capture essences, his poems express the same themes and world view as *cante jondo*, and they recreate a tapestry of Andalusia's mystery and pain. The true Andalusia, the one lying just beneath its sun-drenched landscape. What we have here is not some tourist Andalusia filled with happy-go-lucky Gypsies and picturesque whitewashed villages. Lorca has given us a corner of the earth that is populated by dead lovers and lost, wandering souls; where the blade of a knife flashing in the black, the desolate cry, and a millennium of tears expose Andalusia's almost erotic passion for life, and for death.

Carlos Bauer

POEM OF THE DEEP SONG

BALADILLA DE LOS TRES RÍOS

A Salvador Quintero

El río Guadalquivir
va entre naranjos y olivos.
Los dos ríos de Granada
bajan de la nieve al trigo.

¡Ay, amor
que se fue y no vino!

El río Guadalquivir
tiene las barbas granates.
Los dos ríos de Granada,
uno llanto y otro sangre.

¡Ay, amor
que se fue por el aire!

Para los barcos de vela,
Sevilla tiene un camino;
por el agua de Granada
sólo reman los suspiros.

¡Ay, amor
que se fue y no vino!

Guadalquivir, alta torre
y viento en los naranjales.
Darro y Genil, torrecillas
muertas sobre los estanques.

LITTLE BALLAD OF THE THREE RIVERS

To Salvador Quintero

The river Guadalquivir
winds through orange and olive trees.
The two rivers of Granada
descend from the snow to the wheat.

Ay, love
that went away and never returned!

The river Guadalquivir
has whiskers of garnet.
The two rivers of Granada,
one weeping and the other blood.

Ay, love
that went away through the air!

For ships with sail
Sevilla has a route;
in the waters of Granada
only sighs row about.

Ay, love
that went away and never returned!

Guadalquivir, a tall tower
and wind in the orange groves.
Darro and Genil, dead little
towers rising from the lakes.

¡Ay, amor
que se fue por el aire!

¡Quién dirá que el agua lleva
un fuego fatuo de gritos!

¡Ay, amor
que se fue y no vino!

Lleva azahar, lleva olivas,
Andalucía, a tus mares.

¡Ay, amor
que se fue por el aire!

Ay, love
that went away through the air!

One could say that the water carries
a will-o'-the-wisp filled with cries!

Ay, love
that went away and never returned!

Carry orange blossom, carry olives,
Andalusia, down to your seas.

Ay, love
that went away through the air!

✿ POEMA DE LA SIGUIRIYA GITANA

A Carlos Morla Vicuña

PAISAJE

El campo
de olivos
se abre y se cierra
como un abanico.
Sobre el olivar
hay un cielo hundido
y una lluvia oscura
de luceros fríos.
Tiembla junco y penumbra
a la orilla del río.
Se riza el aire gris.
Los olivos
están cargados
de gritos.
Una bandada
de pájaros cautivos,
que mueven sus larguísimas
colas en lo sombrío.

✤ POEM OF THE GYPSY *SIGUIRIYA*

To Carlos Morla Vicuña

LANDSCAPE

The field
of olive trees
opens and closes
like a fan.
Above the olive grove
there is a sunken sky
and a dark shower
of cold stars.
Bulrush and twilight tremble
at the edge of the river.
The grey air ripples.
The olive trees
are charged
with cries.
A flock
of captive birds,
shaking their very long
tail feathers in the gloom.

LA GUITARRA

Empieza el llanto
de la guitarra.
Se rompen las copas
de la madrugada.
Empieza el llanto
de la guitarra.
Es inútil
callarla.
Es imposible
callarla.
Llora monótona
como llora el agua,
como llora el viento
sobre la nevada.
Es imposible
callarla.
Llora por cosas
lejanas.
Arena del Sur caliente
que pide camelias blancas.
Llora flecha sin blanco,
la tarde sin mañana,
y el primer pájaro muerto
sobre la rama.
¡Oh guitarra!
Corazón malherido
por cinco espadas.

THE GUITAR

The weeping
of the guitar begins.
Wineglasses shatter
in the dead of night.
The weeping
of the guitar begins.
It's useless
to hush it.
It's impossible
to hush it.
It weeps on monotonously
the way water weeps,
the way wind weeps
over the snowdrifts.
It's impossible
to hush it.
It weeps for things
far, far away.
For the sand of the hot South
that begs for white camellias.
Weeps for arrows without targets,
an afternoon without a morning,
and for the first dead bird
upon the branch.
Oh, guitar!
Heart gravely wounded
by five swords.

EL GRITO

La elipse de un grito
va de monte
a monte.

Desde los olivos,
será un arco iris negro
sobre la noche azul.

¡Ay!

Como un arco de viola,
el grito ha hecho vibrar
largas cuerdas del viento.

¡Ay!

(Las gentes de las cuevas
asoman sus velones.)

¡Ay!

THE CRY

The ellipse of a cry
travels from mountain
to mountain.

From the olive trees
it appears as a black
rainbow upon the blue night.

Ay!

Like the bow of a viola
the cry has made the long
strings of the wind vibrate.

Ay!

(The folks from the caves
stick out their oil lamps.)

Ay!

EL SILENCIO

Oye, hijo mío, el silencio.
Es un silencio ondulado,
un silencio,
donde resbalan valles y ecos
y que inclina las frentes
hacia el suelo.

THE SILENCE

Listen, my son: the silence.
It's a rolling silence,
a silence
where valleys and echoes slip,
and it bends foreheads
down towards the ground.

EL PASO DE LA SIGUIRIYA

Entre mariposas negras,
va una muchacha morena
junto a una blanca serpiente
de niebla.

Tierra de luz,
cielo de tierra.

Va encadenada al temblor
de un ritmo que nunca llega;
tiene el corazón de plata
y un puñal en la diestra.

¿Adónde vas, siguiriya,
con un ritmo sin cabeza?
¿Qué luna recogerá
tu dolor de cal y adelfa?

Tierra de luz,
cielo de tierra.

THE PASSING STAGE OF THE *SIGUIRIYA*

Among black butterflies
goes a dark-haired girl
next to a white serpent
of mist.

Earth of light,
sky of earth.

She is chained to the tremor
of a never arriving rhythm;
she has a heart of silver
and a dagger in her right hand.

Where are you going, *siguiriya,*
with such a headless rhythm?
What moon'll gather up your pain
of whitewash and oleander?

Earth of light,
sky of earth.

DESPUÉS DE PASAR

Los niños miran
un punto lejano.

Los candiles se apagan.
Unas muchachas ciegas
preguntan a la luna,
y por el aire ascienden
espirales de llanto.

Las montañas miran
un punto lejano.

AFTER PASSING BY

The children observe
a point far, far away.

The oil lamps are put out.
Some blind girls
question the moon,
and through the air rise
spirals of weeping.

The mountains observe
a point far, far away.

Y DESPUÉS

Los laberintos
que crea el tiempo,
se desvanecen.

(Sólo queda
el desierto.)

El corazón,
fuente del deseo,
se desvanece.

(Sólo queda
el desierto.)

La ilusión de la aurora
y los besos,
se desvanecen.

Sólo queda
el desierto.
Un ondulado
desierto.

AND AFTER THAT

The labyrinths
that time creates
vanish.

(Only the desert
remains.)

The heart,
fountain of desire,
vanishes.

(Only the desert
remains.)

The illusion of dawn
and kisses
vanish.

Only the desert
remains.
A rolling
desert.

✿ POEMA DE LA SOLEÁ

A Jorge Zalamea

EVOCACIÓN

Tierra seca,
tierra quieta
de noches
inmensas.

(Viento en el olivar,
viento en la sierra.)

Tierra
vieja
del candil
y la pena.
Tierra
de las hondas cisternas.
Tierra
de la muerte sin ojos
y las flechas.

(Viento por los caminos.
Brisa en las alamedas.)

✳ POEM OF THE *SOLEÁ*

To Jorge Zalamea

EVOCATION

Dry land,
still land
of immense
nights.

(Wind in the olive grove,
wind in the sierra.)

Ancient
land
of oil lamp
and grief.
Land
of deep cisterns.
Land
of a death without eyes
and of arrows.

(Wind on the roads.
Breeze in the poplar groves.)

PUEBLO

Sobre el monte pelado,
un calvario.
Agua clara
y olivos centenarios.
Por las callejas
hombres embozados,
y en las torres
veletas girando.
Eternamente
girando.
¡Oh pueblo perdido
en la Andalucía del llanto!

VILLAGE

Upon a barren mount,
a calvary.
Clear water
and century-old olive trees.
In the narrow streets,
men hidden under cloaks;
and on the towers,
weather vanes spinning round.
Eternally
spinning.
Oh, lost village,
in the Andalusia of tears!

PUÑAL

El puñal
entra en el corazón
como la reja del arado
en el yermo.

    No.
  No me lo claves.
    No.

El puñal,
como un rayo de sol,
incendia las terribles
hondonadas.

    No.
  No me lo claves.
    No.

DAGGER

The dagger
enters into the heart
like the ploughshare
into the barren waste.

No.
Don't plunge it into me.
No.

The dagger,
like the sunbeam,
sets ablaze the terrible
hollows.

No.
Don't plunge it into me.
No.

ENCRUCIJADA

Viento del Este,
un farol
y el puñal
en el corazón.
La calle
tiene un temblor
de cuerda
en tensión,
un temblor
de enorme moscardón.
Por todas partes
yo
veo el puñal
en el corazón.

CROSSROADS

East wind,
a streetlamp
and the dagger
in the heart.
The street
has the quiver
of a string
pulled tight,
the quiver
of a huge horsefly.
Everywhere
I
see the dagger
in the heart.

¡AY!

El grito deja en el viento
una sombra de ciprés.

(Dejadme en este campo
llorando.)

Todo se ha roto en el mundo.
No queda más que el silencio.

(Dejadme en este campo
llorando.)

El horizonte sin luz
está mordido de hogueras.

(Ya os he dicho que me dejéis
en este campo
llorando.)

AY!

The cry leaves a shadow
of cypress upon the wind.

(Leave me here in this field,
weeping.)

Everything in the world is broken.
Nothing but silence remains.

(Leave me here in this field,
weeping.)

The moonless horizon
is chewed up by bonfires.

(I've told you already to leave me
here in this field,
weeping.)

SORPRESA

Muerto se quedó en la calle
con un puñal en el pecho.
No lo conocía nadie.
¡Cómo temblaba el farol!
Madre.
¡Cómo temblaba el farolito
de la calle!
Era madrugada. Nadie
pudo asomarse a sus ojos
abiertos al duro aire.
Que muerto se quedó en la calle
que con un puñal en el pecho
y que no lo conocía nadie.

SURPRISE

Dead he was left in the street,
with a dagger in his chest.
Nobody knew who he was.
How the lamppost was shaking!
Mother.
How that little lamppost shook
in the street!
In the dead of night. Nobody
was able to glance wide-eyed
out into the harsh night air.
And he was left dead in the street,
and with a dagger in his chest,
and nobody knew who he was.

LA SOLEÁ

Vestida con mantos negros
piensa que el mundo es chiquito
y el corazón es inmenso.

Vestida con mantos negros.

Piensa que el suspiro tierno
y el grito, desaparecen
en la corriente del viento.

Vestida con mantos negros.

Se dejó el balcón abierto
y al alba por el balcón
desembocó todo el cielo.

¡Ay yayayayay,
que vestida con mantos negros!

THE *SOLEÁ*

Dressed in black mantles,
she thinks the world is tiny
and the heart immense.

Dressed in black mantles.

She thinks the loving sigh
and the cry disappear
on the currents of the wind.

Dressed in black mantles.

The balcony was left open
and at dawn the whole sky
emptied onto the balcony.

Ay yayayayay,
dressed in black mantles!

CUEVA

De la cueva salen
largos sollozos.

(Lo cárdeno
sobre lo rojo.)

El gitano evoca
países remotos.

(Torres altas y hombres
misteriosos.)

En la voz entrecortada
van sus ojos.

(Lo negro
sobre lo rojo.)

Y la cueva encalada
tiembla en el oro.

(Lo blanco
sobre lo rojo.)

CAVE

From the cave come
long sobs.

(The purple
over the red.)

The Gypsy evokes
remote lands.

(High towers and men
of mystery.)

Over the cracking voice
his eyes travel.

(The black
over the red.)

And the whitewashed cave
trembles in gold.

(The white
over the red.)

ENCUENTRO

Ni tú ni yo estamos
en disposición
de encontrarnos.
Tú...por lo que ya sabes.
¡Yo la he querido tanto!
Sigue esa veredita.
En las manos
tengo los agujeros
de los clavos.
¿No ves cómo me estoy
desangrando?
No mires nunca atrás,
vete despacio
y reza como yo
a San Cayetano,
que ni tú ni yo estamos
en disposición
de encontrarnos.

ENCOUNTER

Neither you nor I are
ready
to find one another.
You...for reasons you know.
I loved her so much!
Follow that narrow path.
In my hands
I've got holes
from the nails.
Can't you see how
I'm bleeding to death?
Never glance back,
continue on slowly
and pray the way I do,
to San Cayetano,
for neither you nor I are
ready
to find one another.

ALBA

Campanas de Córdoba
en la madrugada.
Campanas de amanecer
en Granada.
Os sienten todas las muchachas
que lloran a la tierna
soleá enlutada.
Las muchachas
de Andalucía la alta
y la baja.
Las niñas de España,
de pie menudo
y temblorosas faldas,
que han llenado de cruces
las encrucijadas.
¡Oh campanas de Córdoba
en la madrugada,
y oh campanas de amanecer
en Granada!

DAWN

Bells of Córdoba
before daybreak.
Bells of dawn
in Granada.
You're heard by all the girls
who weep to the tender,
grieving *soleá*.
The girls
of upper Andalusia
and of lower.
The young girls of Spain,
tiny of foot
and with trembling skirts,
who've filled the crossroads
with crosses.
Oh, bells of Córdoba
before daybreak,
and, oh, bells of dawn
in Granada!

✿ POEMA DE LA SAETA

A Francisco Iglesias

ARQUEROS

Los arqueros oscuros
a Sevilla se acercan.

Guadalquivir abierto.

Anchos sombreros grises,
largas capas lentas.

¡Ay, Guadalquivir!

Vienen de los remotos
países de la pena.

Guadalquivir abierto.

Y van a un laberinto.
Amor, cristal y piedra.

¡Ay, Guadalquivir!

℘ POEM OF THE *SAETA*

To Francisco Iglesias

ARCHERS

The dark archers
approach Sevilla.

Open Guadalquivir.

Broad, grey hats;
long, sluggish capes.

Ay, Guadalquivir!

They come from remote
countries of sorrow.

Open Guadalquivir.

And they're entering a labyrinth.
Love, crystal and stone.

Ay, Guadalquivir!

NOCHE

Cirio, candil,
farol y luciérnaga.

La constelación
de la saeta.

Ventanitas de oro
tiemblan,
y en la aurora se mecen
cruces superpuestas.

Cirio, candil,
farol y luciérnaga.

NIGHT

Candle, oil lamp,
lamppost and firefly.

The constellation
of the *saeta*.

Little golden windows
tremble,
and at dawn superimposed
crosses sway about.

Candle, oil lamp,
lamppost and firefly.

SEVILLA

Sevilla es una torre
llena de arqueros finos.

Sevilla para herir.
Córdoba para morir.

Una ciudad que acecha
largos ritmos,
y los enrosca
como laberintos.
Como tallos de parra
encendidos.

¡Sevilla para herir!

Bajo el arco del cielo,
sobre su llano limpio,
dispara la constante
saeta de su río.

¡Córdoba para morir!

Y loca de horizonte,
mezcla en su vino
lo amargo de Don Juan
y lo perfecto de Dionisio.

Sevilla para herir.
¡Siempre Sevilla para herir!

SEVILLA

Sevilla is a tower
full of fine archers.

Sevilla to wound.
Córdoba to die.

A city lying in ambush
for long rhythms,
and it coils them up
like labyrinths.
Like flaming
grapevine stems.

Sevilla to wound!

Beneath the sky's arch,
above its clean plain,
it shoots the constant
arrow of its river.

Córdoba to die!

And crazed by the horizon,
it mixes in its own wine
the bitterness of Don Juan
and the perfection of Dionysius.

Sevilla to wound.
Forever Sevilla to wound!

PROCESIÓN

Por la calleja vienen
extraños unicornios.
¿De qué campo,
de qué bosque mitológico?
Más cerca,
ya parecen astrónomos.
Fantásticos Merlines
y el Ecce Homo,
Durandarte encantado,
Orlando furioso.

PROCESSION

Down the narrow street
come strange unicorns.
From what field,
from what mythical forest?
Closer still,
now they appear to be astronomers.
Fantastic Merlins
and the Ecce Homo,
an enchanted Durandarte,
a furious Orlando.

PASO

Virgen con miriñaque,
virgen de la Soledad,
abierta como un inmenso
tulipán.
En un barco de luces
vas
por la alta marea
de la ciudad,
entre saetas turbias
y estrellas de cristal.
Virgen con miriñaque,
tú vas
por el río de la calle,
¡hasta el mar!

STAGE

Virgin in crinoline,
virgin of Solitude,
opened up like an immense
tulip.
In a boat of light,
you travel
upon the high tide
of the city,
among turbid *saetas*
and stars of crystal.
Virgin in crinoline,
you travel
on that river of a street—
down to the sea!

SAETA

Cristo moreno
pasa
de lirio de Judea
a clavel de España.

¡Miradlo por dónde viene!

De España.
Cielo limpio y oscuro,
tierra tostada,
y cauces donde corre
muy lenta el agua.
Cristo moreno,
con las guedejas quemadas,
los pómulos salientes
y las pupilas blancas.

¡Miradlo por dónde va!

SAETA

A dark Christ
changes
from a lily of Judea
to a carnation of Spain.

Look where he comes from!

From Spain.
A dark and clear sky,
a toasted earth,
and riverbeds where water
runs ever so slowly.
A dark Christ,
with long, burnt locks;
his cheekbones, prominent
and his pupils, white.

Look where he's going!

BALCÓN

La Lola
canta saetas.
Los toreritos
la rodean,
y el barberillo,
desde su puerta,
sigue los ritmos
con la cabeza.
Entre la albahaca
y la hierbabuena,
la Lola canta
saetas.
La Lola aquella,
que se miraba
tanto en la alberca.

BALCONY

Lola
is singing *saetas*.
The little bullfighters
circle around her;
and the little barber,
from his doorway,
follows the rhythm
with his head.
Among sweet basil
and mint,
Lola is singing
saetas.
That Lola,
who would look at herself
so much in the pool.

MADRUGADA

Pero como el amor
los saeteros
están ciegos.

Sobre la noche verde,
las saetas
dejan rastros de lirio
caliente.

La quilla de la luna
rompe nubes moradas
y las aljabas
se llenan de rocío.

¡Ay, pero como el amor
los saeteros
están ciegos!

BEFORE THE DAWN

But like love
the archers
are blind

Upon the green night,
the piercing *saetas*
leave traces of warm
lily.

The keel of the moon
breaks through purple clouds
and their quivers
fill with dew.

Ay, but like love
the archers
are blind!

✖ GRÁFICO DE LA PETENERA

A Eugenio Montes

CAMPANA

BORDÓN

En la torre
amarilla,
dobla una campana.

Sobre el viento
amarillo,
se abren las campanadas.

En la torre
amarilla,
cesa la campana.

El viento con el polvo
hace proras de plata.

❧ SKETCH OF THE *PETENERA*

To Eugenio Montes

BELL

BASS STRING

In the yellow
tower,
a bell tolls.

Upon the yellow
wind,
ringing breaks out.

In the yellow
tower,
the bell stops.

The wind, with the dust,
creates prows of silver.

CAMINO

Cien jinetes enlutados,
¿dónde irán,
por el cielo yacente
del naranjal?
Ni a Córdoba ni a Sevilla
llegarán.
Ni a Granada la que suspira
por el mar.
Esos caballos soñolientos
los llevarán,
al laberinto de las cruces
donde tiembla el cantar.
Con siete ayes clavados,
¿dónde irán
los cien jinetes andaluces
del naranjal?

ROAD

A hundred riders in funeral dress,
where will they go
in that laid-to-rest sky
of the orange grove?
Neither Córdoba nor Sevilla
will they ever reach.
Nor that Granada which sighs
for the sea.
Those drowsy horses
will carry them:
to that labyrinth of crosses
where the song shudders so.
With seven *ays* piercing them,
where will they go,
those hundred Andalusian riders
of the orange grove?

LAS SEIS CUERDAS

La guitarra
hace llorar a los sueños.
El sollozo de las almas
perdidas
se escapa por su boca
redonda.
Y como la tarántula
teje una gran estrella
para cazar suspiros,
que flotan en su negro
aljibe de madera.

THE SIX STRINGS

The guitar
makes dreams weep.
The sobbing of lost
souls
escapes through its round
mouth.
And like the tarantula
it spins a large star
to trap the sighs
floating in its black,
wooden water tank.

DANZA

En la noche del huerto,
seis gitanas
vestidas de blanco
bailan.

En la noche del huerto,
coronadas
con rosas de papel
y biznagas.

En la noche del huerto,
sus dientes de nácar
escriben la sombra
quemada.

Y en la noche de huerto,
sus sombras se alargan,
y llegan hasta el cielo
moradas.

DANCE

In the garden's night,
six Gypsy girls,
dressed in white,
are dancing.

In the garden's night,
crowned
with paper roses
and bishop's weed.

In the garden's night,
their mother-of-pearl teeth
score the charred
shadow.

In the garden's night,
their shadows lengthen
and reach up to the sky
with a purplish color.

MUERTE DE LA PETENERA

En la casa blanca muere
la perdición de los hombres.

Cien jacas caracolean.
Sus jinetes están muertos.

Bajo las estremecidas
estrellas de los velones,
su falda de moaré tiembla
entre sus muslos de cobre.

Cien jacas caracolean.
Sus jinetes están muertos.

Largas sombras afiladas
vienen del turbio horizonte,
y el bordón de una guitarra
se rompe.

Cien jacas caracolean.
Sus jinetes están muertos.

DEATH OF THE *PETENERA*

In this white house,
man's perdition dies.

A hundred ponies are prancing.
Their riders are all dead.

Beneath the quivering
stars of the oil lamps,
her skirt of moire trembles
between her copper thighs.

A hundred ponies are prancing.
Their riders are all dead.

Long, sharpened shadows
come from the cloudy horizon,
and the bass string of a guitar
breaks.

A hundred ponies are prancing.
Their riders are all dead.

FALSETA

¡Ay, petenera gitana!
¡Yayay petenera!
Tu entierro no tuvo niñas
buenas.
Niñas que le dan a Cristo muerto
sus guedejas,
y llevan blancas mantillas
en las ferias.
Tu entierro fue de gente
siniestra.
Gente con el corazón
en la cabeza,
que te siguió llorando
por las callejas.
¡Ay, petenera gitana!
¡Yayay petenera!

GUITAR FLOURISH

Ay, Gypsy *petenera!*
Yayay, petenera!
There weren't any good little girls
at your burial.
Little girls who offer a dead Christ
their locks,
and who wear white mantillas
on market days.
Your burial was one of sinister
people.
People with their hearts
in their heads;
who followed after you, weeping
through the narrow streets.
Ay, Gypsy *petenera!*
Yayay, petenera!

DE PROFUNDIS

Los cien enamorados
duermen para siempre
bajo la tierra seca.
Andalucía tiene
largos caminos rojos.
Córdoba, olivos verdes
donde poner cien cruces,
que los recuerden.
Los cien enamorados
duermen para siempre.

DE PROFUNDIS

Those hundred lovers
are asleep forever
beneath the dry earth.
Andalusia has
long, red-colored roads.
Córdoba, green olive trees
for placing a hundred crosses
to remember them.
Those hundred lovers
are asleep forever.

CLAMOR

En las torres
amarillas,
doblan las campanas.

Sobre los vientos
amarillos,
se abren las campanadas.

Por un camino va
la Muerte, coronada
de azahares marchitos.
Canta y canta
una canción
en su vihuela blanca,
y canta y canta y canta.

En las torres amarillas,
cesan las campanas.

El viento con el polvo
hacen proras de plata.

DEATH KNELL

In the yellow
towers,
the bells toll.

Upon the yellow
winds,
ringing breaks out.

Down a road travels
Death, crowned with
withered orange blossoms.
Death sings and sings
a song
with her ancient white guitar,
and sings and sings and sings.

In the yellow towers,
the bells stop.

The wind and the dust
create prows of silver.

❧ DOS MUCHACHAS

A Máximo Quijano

LA LOLA

Bajo el naranjo lava
pañales de algodón.
Tiene verdes los ojos
y violeta la voz.

¡Ay, amor,
bajo el naranjo en flor!

El agua de la acequia
iba llena de sol,
en el olivarito
cantaba un gorrión.

¡Ay, amor,
bajo el naranjo en flor!

Luego, cuando la Lola
gaste todo el jabón,
vendrán los torerillos.

¡Ay, amor,
bajo el naranjo en flor!

❦ TWO YOUNG GIRLS

To Máximo Quijano

LOLA

Under the orange tree, she
washes cotton diapers.
Her eyes are green
and violet, her voice.

Ay, love,
under the orange tree in flower!

The water of the irrigation canal
was moving along filled with sun;
in the little olive grove,
a sparrow was singing.

Ay, love,
under the orange tree in flower!

Later, when Lola
uses up all her soap,
the little bullfighters arrive.

Ay, love,
under the orange tree in flower!

AMPARO

Amparo,
¡qué sola estás en tu casa
vestida de blanco!

(Ecuador entre el jazmín
y el nardo.)

Oyes los maravillosos
surtidores de tu patio,
y el débil trino amarillo
del canario.

Por la tarde ves temblar
los cipreses con los pájaros,
mientras bordas lentamente
letras sobre el cañamazo.

Amparo,
¡qué sola estás en tu casa
vestida de blanco!
Amparo,
¡y qué difícil decirte:
yo te amo!

AMPARO

Amparo,
how lonely you are at home,
dressed in white!

(Dividing line between jasmine
and spikenard.)

You hear the wonderful
fountains of your courtyard
and the weak, yellow trilling
of the canary.

In the evening, you see
the cypresses shake with birds
while you slowly embroider
letters into the canvas.

Amparo,
how lonely you are at home,
dressed in white!
Amparo,
and how difficult to tell you:
I love you!

❦ VIÑETAS FLAMENCAS

A Manuel Torres, «Niño de Jerez»,
que tiene tronco de Faraón.

RETRATO DE SILVERIO FRANCONETTI

Entre italiano
y flamenco,
¿cómo cantaría
aquel Silverio?
La densa miel de Italia,
con el limón nuestro,
iba en el hondo llanto
del siguiriyero.
Su grito fue terrible.
Los viejos
dicen que se erizaban
los cabellos,
y se abría el azogue
de los espejos.
Pasaba por los tonos
sin romperlos.
Y fue un creador
y un jardinero.
Un creador de glorietas
para el silencio.

Ahora su melodía
duerme con los ecos.
Definitiva y pura.
¡Con los últimos ecos!

❧ FLAMENCO VIGNETTES

To Manuel Torres, "Niño de Jerez,"
who has the body of a Pharaoh.

PORTRAIT OF SILVERIO FRANCONETTI

Between Italian
and flamenco,
how would he sing,
that Silverio?
The thick honey of Italy,
mixed with our lemon,
traveled upon the deep wail
of this singer of *siguiriyas*.
His cry was terrible.
Old timers say
that one's hair
would stand on end,
and make the quicksilver
split in the mirrors.
He would go up the scales
without his voice cracking.
And he was a creator
and a gardener.
A creator of arbors
for the silence.

Now his melody
sleeps with the echoes.
Final and pure.
With the ultimate echoes!

JUAN BREVA

Juan Breva tenía
cuerpo de gigante
y voz de niña.
Nada como su trino.
Era la misma
Pena cantando
detrás de una sonrisa.
Evoca los limonares
de Málaga la dormida,
y hay en su llanto dejos
de sal marina.
Como Homero cantó
ciego. Su voz tenía
algo de mar sin luz
y naranja exprimida.

JUAN BREVA

Juan Breva possessed
the body of a giant
and the voice of a little girl.
His trill was like nothing else.
It was that same Pain
being sung
behind a smile.
It evokes the lemon groves
of a sleepy Málaga,
and in his wail there are
aftertastes of sea salt.
Like Homer he sang
blindly. His voice possessed
a touch of sea without light
and squeezed-dry orange.

CAFÉ CANTANTE

Lámparas de cristal
y espejos verdes.

Sobre el tablado oscuro,
la Parrala sostiene
una conversación
con la Muerte.
La llama,
no viene,
y la vuelve a llamar.
Las gentes
aspiran los sollozos.
Y en los espejos verdes,
largas colas de seda
se mueven.

FLAMENCO CABARET

Lamps of crystal
and green mirrors.

On the darkened stage,
Parrala maintains
a conversation
with Death.
She calls Death,
but Death never comes,
and she calls out again.
The people are
inhaling her sobs.
And in the green mirrors,
her long, silk train
sways back and forth.

LAMENTACIÓN DE LA MUERTE

A Miguel Benítez

Sobre el cielo negro,
culebrinas amarillas.

Vine a este mundo con ojos
y me voy sin ellos.
¡Señor del mayor dolor!
Y luego,
un velón y una manta
en el suelo.

Quise llegar adonde
llegaron los buenos.
¡Y he llegado, Dios mío!...
Pero luego,
un velón y una manta
en el suelo.

Limoncito amarillo,
limonero.
Echad los limoncitos
al viento.
¡Ya lo sabéis!...Porque luego,
luego,
un velón y una manta
en el suelo.

Sobre el cielo negro,
culebrinas amarillas.

LAMENTATION OF DEATH

To Miguel Benítez

Across the black heavens,
yellow, serpentine flashes.

I came into this world with eyes
and I'll leave without them.
Oh, Lord of the greatest sorrow!
And then,
an oil lamp and a blanket
upon the ground.

I tried to go where
the good people go.
And I did, dear God...!
But then,
an oil lamp and a blanket
upon the ground.

Little yellow lemons,
lemon tree.
Cast your little lemons
to the wind.
Now you know...! For then,
then,
an oil lamp and a blanket
upon the ground.

Across the black heavens,
yellow, serpentine flashes.

CONJURO

La mano crispada
como una Medusa
ciega el ojo doliente
del candil.

As de bastos.
Tijeras en cruz.

Sobre el humo blanco
del incienso, tiene
algo de topo y
mariposa indecisa.

As de bastos.
Tijeras en cruz.

Aprieta un corazón
invisible, ¿la veis?
Un corazón
reflejado en el viento.

As de bastos.
Tijeras en cruz.

INCANTATION

The twitching hand,
like some Medusa,
blinds the aching eye
of the oil lamp.

Ace of Wands.
Scissors in a cross.

Upon the white smoke
of the incense, it has
a touch of the mole and
the indecisive butterfly.

Ace of Wands.
Scissors in a cross.

An invisible heart
is distressed, see it?
A heart
reflected on the wind.

Ace of Wands.
Scissors in a cross.

MEMENTO

Cuando yo me muera,
enterradme con mi guitarra
bajo la arena.

Cuando yo me muera,
entre los naranjos
y la hierbabuena.

Cuando yo me muera,
enterradme si queréis
en una veleta.

¡Cuando yo me muera!

MEMENTO

When I die,
bury me with my guitar
beneath the sand.

When I die,
among orange trees
and mint plants.

When I die,
bury me, if you would,
inside a weather vane.

When I die!

❧ TRES CIUDADES

A Pilar Zubiaurre

MALAGUEÑA

La muerte
entra y sale
de la taberna.

Pasan caballos negros
y gente siniestra
por los hondos caminos
de la guitarra.

Y hay un olor a sal
y a sangre de hembra
en los nardos febriles
de la marina.

La muerte
entra y sale,
y sale y entra
la muerte
de la taberna.

❧ THREE CITIES

To Pilar Zubiaurre

MALAGUEÑA

Death
goes in and out
of the tavern.

Black horses
and sinister people
travel the deep roads
of the guitar.

And there's a smell of salt
and of female blood
in the feverish nards
along the seacoast.

Death
goes in and out;
and out and into
the tavern
goes death.

BARRIO DE CÓRDOBA

TÓPICO NOCTURNO

En la casa se defienden
de las estrellas.
La noche se derrumba.
Dentro, hay una niña muerta
con una rosa encarnada
oculta en la cabellera.
Seis ruiseñores la lloran
en la reja.

Las gentes van suspirando
con las guitarras abiertas.

NEIGHBORHOOD IN CÓRDOBA

NOCTURNAL THEME

In the house, they defend
against the stars.
The night tumbles down.
Inside is a dead little girl
with a flesh-colored rose
hidden in her hair.
Six nightingales sing to her
from the bars of the window.

The folks are sighing
with their guitars open.

BAILE

La Carmen está bailando
por las calles de Sevilla.
Tiene blancos los cabellos
y brillantes las pupilas.

¡Niñas,
corred las cortinas!

En su cabeza se enrosca
una serpiente amarilla,
y va soñando en el baile
con galanes de otros días.

¡Niñas,
corred las cortinas!

Las calles están desiertas
y en los fondos se adivinan
corazones andaluces
buscando viejas espinas.

¡Niñas,
corred las cortinas!

DANCE

Carmen is dancing through
the streets of Sevilla.
Her tresses are white
and her pupils, gleaming.

Girls,
shut the curtains!

In her head, a yellow
serpent is coiling up,
and she dreams about dancing
with suitors from days gone by.

Girls,
shut the curtains!

The streets are deserted,
and Andalusian hearts
in search of ancient thorns
are detected in the background.

Girls,
shut the curtains!

SEIS CAPRICHOS

A Regino Sainz de la Maza

ADIVINANZA DE LA GUITARRA

En la redonda
encrucijada,
seis doncellas
bailan.
Tres de carne
y tres de plata.
Los sueños de ayer las buscan,
pero las tiene abrazadas
un Polifemo de oro.
¡La guitarra!

❄ SIX CAPRICES

To Regino Sainz de la Maza

RIDDLE OF THE GUITAR

In the round
crossroads,
six maidens
are dancing.
Three of flesh
and three of silver.
Yesterday's dreams search for them,
but a golden Polyphemus
is embracing them.
The guitar!

CANDIL

¡Oh, qué grave medita
la llama del candil!

Como un faquir indio
mira su entraña de oro
y se eclipsa soñando
atmósferas sin viento.

Cigüeña incandescente
pica desde su nido
a las sombras macizas,
y se asoma temblando
a los ojos redondos
del gitanillo muerto.

OIL LAMP

Oh, how gravely the flame
of the oil lamp meditates!

Like an Indian fakir
it stares at its golden navel
and then is eclipsed, dreaming
of windless atmospheres.

An incandescent stork
pecks at the plump shadows
from inside its nest
and, trembling, peeks
into the round eyes
of a dead little Gypsy.

CRÓTALO

Crótalo.
Crótalo.
Crótalo.
Escarabajo sonoro.

En la araña
de la mano
rizas el aire
cálido,
y te ahogas en tu trino
de palo.

Crótalo.
Crótalo.
Crótalo.
Escarabajo sonoro.

CASTANET

Rattler.
Rattler.
Rattler.
Sonorous beetle.

In the spider
of the hand,
you ripple the warm
air
and drown in your trill
of wood.

Rattler.
Rattler.
Rattler.
Sonorous beetle.

CHUMBERA

Laoconte salvaje.

¡Qué bien estás
bajo la media luna!

Múltiple pelotari.

¡Qué bien estás
amenazando al viento!

Dafne y Atis,
saben de tu dolor.
Inexplicable.

PRICKLY PEAR

Wild laocoon.

How comfortable you are
beneath the half-moon!

Multiple pelota player.

How comfortable you are,
threatening the wind!

Daphne and Attis
know of your pain.
Inexplicable.

PITA

Pulpo petrificado.

Pones cinchas cenicientas
al vientre de los montes,
y muelas formidables
a los desfiladeros.

Pulpo petrificado.

MAGUEY PLANT

Petrified octopus.

You put ashen cinches on
the bellies of mountains
and formidable molars
into their high passes.

Petrified octopus.

CRUZ

La cruz.
(Punto final
del camino.)

Se mira en la acequia.
(Puntos suspensivos.)

CROSS

The cross.
(The full stop
of one's road.)

It looks at itself in the canal.
(Suspension points.)

ESCENA DEL TENIENTE CORONEL DE LA GUARDIA CIVIL

CUARTO DE BANDERAS

TENIENTE CORONEL: Yo soy el teniente coronel de la Guardia Civil.

SARGENTO: Sí.

TENIENTE CORONEL: Y no hay quien me desmienta.

SARGENTO: No.

TENIENTE CORONEL: Tengo tres estrellas y veinte cruces.

SARGENTO: Sí.

TENIENTE CORONEL: Me ha saludado el cardenal arzobispo de Toledo con sus veinticuatro borlas moradas.

SARGENTO: Sí.

TENIENTE CORONEL: Yo soy el teniente. Yo soy el teniente. Yo soy el teniente coronel de la Guardia Civil.

(Romeo y Julieta, celeste, blanco y oro, se abrazan sobre el jardín de tabaco de la caja de puros. El militar acaricia el cañón de un fusil lleno de sombra submarina.)

UNA VOZ (*Fuera*): Luna, luna, luna, luna,
                del tiempo de la aceituna.
                Cazorla enseña su torre
                y Benamejí la oculta.

SCENE OF THE LIEUTENANT COLONEL OF THE CIVIL GUARD

GUARDROOM

LT. COLONEL: I'm the Lieutenant Colonel of the Civil Guard.

SERGEANT: Yes, sir.

LT. COLONEL: And there's nobody who'll contradict me.

SERGEANT: No, sir.

LT. COLONEL: I've got three stars and twenty crosses.

SERGEANT: Yes, sir.

LT. COLONEL: The Cardinal Archbishop of Toledo greeted me in his twenty-four purple tassels.

SERGEANT: Yes, sir.

LT. COLONEL: I'm the Lieutenant. I'm the Lieutenant. I'm the Lieutenant Colonel of the Civil Guard.

(Romeo and Juliet — in the sky blue, white and gold — embrace upon the tobacco garden of the cigar box. The military man caresses the barrel of a gun filled with submarine shadows.)

A VOICE: *(off stage):* The moon, moon, moon, moon,
of the olive's harvest moon.
Cazorla, her tower she reveals,
which Benamejí then conceals.

107

Luna, luna, luna, luna.
Un gallo canta en la luna.
Señor alcalde, sus niñas
están mirando a la luna.

TENIENTE CORONEL: ¿Qué pasa?

SARGENTO: ¡Un gitano!

(*La mirada de mulo joven del gitanillo ensombrece
y agiganta los ojirris del* Teniente Coronel *de la*
Guardia Civil.)

TENIENTE CORONEL: Yo soy el teniente coronel de la
Guardia Civil.

GITANO: Sí.

TENIENTE CORONEL: ¿Tú quién eres?

GITANO: Un gitano.

TENIENTE CORONEL: ¿Y qué es un gitano?

GITANO: Cualquier cosa.

TENIENTE CORONEL: ¿Cómo te llamas?

GITANO: Eso.

TENIENTE CORONEL: ¿Qué dices?

GITANO: Gitano.

The moon, moon, moon, moon.
A rooster sings in the moon.
Mr. Mayor, your little girls
are looking up at the moon.

LT. COLONEL: What's going on?

SERGEANT: A Gypsy!

*(The mulish gaze of the young little Gypsy makes the
beady little eyes of the* Lt. Colonel *of the Civil Guard
widen and darken.)*

LT. COLONEL: I'm the Lieutenant Colonel of the Civil Guard.

GYPSY: Yes, sir.

LT. COLONEL: And you, who are you?

GYPSY: A Gypsy.

LT. COLONEL: And what's a Gypsy?

GYPSY: Anything at all.

LT. COLONEL: What do they call you?

GYPSY: Just that.

LT. COLONEL: What are you saying?

GYPSY: Gypsy.

SARGENTO: Me lo encontré y lo he traído.

TENIENTE CORONEL: ¿Dónde estabas?

GITANO: En el puente de los ríos

TENIENTE CORONEL: Pero ¿de qué ríos?

GITANO: De todos los ríos.

TENIENTE CORONEL: ¿Y qué hacías allí?

GITANO: Una torre de canela.

TENIENTE CORONEL: ¡Sargento!

SARGENTO: A la orden, mi teniente coronel de la Guardia Civil.

GITANO: He inventado unas alas para volar, y vuelo. Azufre y rosa en mis labios.

TENIENTE CORONEL: ¡Ay!

GITANO: Aunque no necesito alas, porque vuelo sin ellas. Nubes y anillos en mi sangre.

TENIENTE CORONEL: ¡Ayy!

GITANO: En enero tengo azahar.

TENIENTE CORONEL (*Retorciéndose*): ¡Ayyyyy!

GITANO: Y naranjas en la nieve.

SERGEANT: I found him and brought him here.

LT. COLONEL: Where were you?

GYPSY: On the bridge over the rivers.

LT. COLONEL: But, over what rivers?

GYPSY: Over all the rivers.

LT. COLONEL: What were you doing there?

GYPSY: Building a tower of cinnamon.

LT. COLONEL: Sergeant!

SERGEANT: At your command, Lieutenant Colonel of the Civil Guard, sir.

GYPSY: I've invented some wings for flying, and I fly all over. Sulphur and rose upon my lips.

LT. COLONEL: Ay!

GYPSY: Though I don't need wings, because I can fly without them. Clouds and rings are in my blood.

LT. COLONEL: Ayy!

GYPSY: In January, I've got orange blossoms.

LT. COLONEL (*backing away*): Ayyyyy!

GYPSY: And oranges in the falling snow.

TENIENTE CORONEL: ¡Ayyyyy! (*Pun, pin, pam. Cae muerto.*)

(*El alma de tabaco y café con leche del* Teniente
Coronel *de la Guardia Civil sale por la ventana.*)

SARGENTO: ¡Socorro!

(*En el patio del cuartel, cuarto guardias civiles
apalean al gitanillo.*)

LT. COLONEL: Ayyyyy! *(Bang, bam, boom. Falls over dead.)*

(The Lieutenant Colonel *of the Civil Guard's soul of tobacco and café au lait sails out the window.)*

SERGEANT: Help!

(In the barracks yard, four civil guards are beating up on the little Gypsy.)

CANCIÓN DEL GITANO APALEADO

Veinticuatro bofetadas.
Veinticinco bofetadas;
después, mi madre, a la noche,
me pondrá en papel de plata.

Guardia civil caminera,
dadme unos sorbitos de agua.
Agua con peces y barcos.
Agua, agua, agua, agua.

¡Ay, mandor de los civiles
que estás arriba en tu sala!
¡No habrá pañuelos de seda
para limpiarme la cara!

5 de julio, 1925

SONG OF THE BEATEN GYPSY

Twenty-four hard blows,
twenty-five hard blows;
later, when it's dark, my mother
will place me on paper of silver.

Civil Guard of the roads,
give me a few sips of water.
Water with fish and boats.
Water, water, water, water.

Ay, listen Civil Guard Commander,
up there above in your chamber.
There'll never be any scarf of lace
for me to clean my bloodied face.

July 5, 1925

DIÁLOGO DEL AMARGO

CAMPO

UNA VOZ: Amargo.
  Las adelfas de mi patio.
  Corazón de almendra amarga.
  Amargo.

(Llegan tres jóvenes con anchos sombreros.)

JOVEN 1.º: Vamos a llegar tarde.

JOVEN 2.º: La noche se nos echa encima.

JOVEN 1.º: ¿Y ése?

JOVEN 2.º: Viene detrás.

JOVEN 1.º*(En alta voz):* ¡Amargo!

AMARGO *(Lejos):* Ya voy.

JOVEN 2.º*(A voces):* ¡Amargo!

AMARGO *(Con calma):* ¡Ya voy!

(Pausa.)

JOVEN 1º: ¡Qué hermosos olivares!

JOVEN 2º: Sí.

(Largo silencio.)

DIALOGUE OF AMARGO, THE BITTER ONE

COUNTRYSIDE

A VOICE: Amargo, bitter one.
  The oleander of my courtyard.
  A heart of bitter almonds.
  Amargo, bitter one.

(Three young men with wide-brimmed hats arrive.)

1st YOUTH: We're going to get there late.

2nd YOUTH: Night is falling all around us.

1st YOUTH: And him?

2nd YOUTH: He's coming along in back of us.

1st YOUTH *(in a loud voice)*: Amargo!

AMARGO *(far off)*: I'm coming.

2nd YOUTH *(shouting)*: Amargo!

AMARGO *(calmly)*: I'm coming!

(Pause.)

1st YOUTH: What beautiful olive groves!

2nd YOUTH: Yes.

(A long silence.)

117

JOVEN 1º: No me gusta andar de noche.

JOVEN 2º: Ni a mí tampoco.

JOVEN 1º: La noche se hizo para dormir.

JOVEN 2º: Es verdad.

(Ranas y grillos hacen la glorieta del estío andaluz.
El Amargo camina con las manos en la cintura.)

AMARGO: Ay yayayay.
Yo le pregunté a la Muerte.
Ay yayayay.

(El grito de su canto pone un acento circunflejo
sobre el corazón de los que le han oído.)

JOVEN 1º *(Desde muy lejos)*: ¡Amargo!

JOVEN 2º *(Casi perdido)*: ¡Amargooo!

(Silencio.)

(El Amargo está solo en medio de la carretera.
Entorna sus grandes ojos verdes y se ciñe la
chaqueta de pana alrededor del talle. Altas
montañas le rodean. Su gran reloj de plata le
suena oscuramente en el bolsillo a cada paso.)

(Un Jinete viene galopando por la carretera.)

JINETE: *(Parando el caballo)* ¡Buenas noches!

1st YOUTH: I don't like traveling at night.

2nd YOUTH: Neither do I.

1st YOUTH: Night was only made for sleeping.

2nd YOUTH: That's true.

(*Frogs and crickets make up this arbor of the Andalusian summertime. Amargo walks with his hands on his hips.*)

AMARGO: Ay yayayay.
      I asked Death a question.
      Ay yayayay.

(*The cry of his song puts a circumflex over the hearts of the two who have heard him.*)

1st YOUTH (*from very far off*): Amargo!

2nd YOUTH (*almost lost*): Amargooo!

(*Silence.*)

(*Amargo is alone in the middle of the road. He half-closes his large green eyes, and pulls his corduroy jacket tight around his waist. High mountains surround him. His large silver watch ticks darkly with his every step.*)

(*A rider comes galloping down the road.*)

RIDER (*stopping the horse*): Good Evening!

AMARGO: A la paz de Dios.

JINETE: ¿Va usted a Granada?

AMARGO: A Granada voy.

JINETE: Pues vamos juntos.

AMARGO: Eso parece.

JINETE: ¿Por qué no monta en la grupa?

AMARGO: Porque no me duelen los pies.

JINETE: Yo vengo de Málaga.

AMARGO: Bueno.

JINETE: Allí están mis hermanos.

AMARGO (Displicente): ¿Cuántos?

JINETE: Son tres. Venden cuchillos. Ese es el negocio.

AMARGO: De salud les sirva.

JINETE: De plata y de oro.

AMARGO: Un cuchillo no tiene que ser más que cuchillo.

JINETE: Se equivoca.

AMARGO: Gracias.

AMARGO: With God's peace.

RIDER: Are you heading to Granada?

AMARGO: To Granada, I'm heading.

RIDER: Well, we'll be going together.

AMARGO: So it seems.

RIDER: Why don't you climb up on back?

AMARGO: Because my feet aren't sore.

RIDER: I'm coming from Málaga.

AMARGO: That's nice.

RIDER: My brothers are there.

AMARGO (*indifferently*): How many?

RIDER: There are three of them. They sell knives. That's their business.

AMARGO: May it bring them good health.

RIDER: Gold and silver ones.

AMARGO: A knife is a knife and nothing more than that.

RIDER: You're mistaken.

AMARGO: Thanks for telling me.

JINETE: Los cuchillos de oro se van solos al corazón. Los de plata cortan el cuello como una brizna de hierba.

AMARGO: ¿No sirven para partir el pan?

JINETE: Los hombres parten el pan con las manos.

AMARGO: ¡Es verdad!

(El caballo se inquieta.)

JINETE: ¡Caballo!

AMARGO: Es la noche.

(El camino ondulante salomoniza la sombra del animal.)

JINETE: ¿Quieres un cuchillo?

AMARGO: No.

JINETE: Mira que te lo regalo.

AMARGO: Pero yo no lo acepto.

JINETE: No tendrás otra ocasión.

AMARGO: ¿Quién sabe?

JINETE: Los otros cuchillos no sirven. Los otros cuchillos son blandos y se asustan de la sangre. Los que nosotros vendemos son fríos. ¿Entiendes? Entran buscando el sitio de más calor y allí se paran.

RIDER: Gold knives go right into the heart by themselves.
Those of silver cut a throat as if it were a blade of grass.

AMARGO: Aren't they good for cutting bread?

RIDER: Men break bread with their hands.

AMARGO: That's true.

(*The horse grows restless.*)

RIDER: Horse!

AMARGO: It's just the night.

(*The rolling road makes the animal's shadow look as if
it were a solomonic column.*)

RIDER: Would you like a knife?

AMARGO: No.

RIDER: Look, I'll give it to you.

AMARGO: But I won't take it.

RIDER: You won't have another chance.

AMARGO: Who knows?

RIDER: Other knives aren't any good. Other knives are soft,
and they're scared of blood. The ones we sell are cold.
Understand? They enter looking for the hottest place,
and there they stop.

(El Amargo *se calla. Su mano derecha se le
enfría como si agarrase un pedazo de oro.)*

JINETE: ¡Qué hermoso cuchillo!

AMARGO: ¿Vale mucho?

JINETE: Pero ¿no quieres éste?

*(Saca un cuchillo de oro. La punta brilla como
una llama de candil.)*

AMARGO: He dicho que no.

JINETE: ¡Muchacho, súbete conmigo!

AMARGO: Todavía no estoy cansado.

(El caballo se vuelve a espantar.)

JINETE: *(Tirando de las bridas):* Pero ¡qué caballo este!

AMARGO: Es lo oscuro.

(Pausa.)

JINETE: Como te iba diciendo, en Málaga están mis tres
hermanos. ¡Qué manera de vender cuchillos! En la catedral
compraron dos mil para adornar todos los altares y poner una
corona a la torre. Muchos barcos escribieron en ellos sus
nombres; los pescadores más humildes de la orilla del mar se
alumbran de noche con el brillo que despiden sus hojas
afiladas.

(Amargo falls silent. His right hand turns cold, as if he were clutching a piece of gold.)

RIDER: What a beautiful knife!

AMARGO: Is it worth a lot?

RIDER: But, wouldn't you like this one?

(He pulls out a gold knife. Its point shines like the flame of an oil lamp.)

AMARGO: I said no.

RIDER: Climb up here with me, boy.

AMARGO: I'm still not tired.

(The horse starts to bolt again.)

RIDER *(pulling the reins)*: But, what a horse this is!

AMARGO: It's only the dark.

(Pause.)

RIDER: As I was telling you, in Málaga are my three brothers. What a way they have of selling knives! At the cathedral they bought two thousand, just so they could adorn all the altars and place a crown upon the tower. Many ships' crews wrote their names into them; the most humble fishermen along the seacoast light up the night with the sparkle given off by their sharp blades.

AMARGO: ¡Es una hermosura!

JINETE: ¿Quién lo puede negar?

(*La noche se espesa como un vino de cien años.*
La serpiente gorda del Sur abre sus ojos en la
madrugada, y hay en los durmientes un deseo
infinito de arrojarse por el balcón a la magia
perversa del perfume y la lejanía.)

AMARGO: Me parece que hemos perdido el camino.

JINETE: (*Parando el caballo*): ¿Sí?

AMARGO: Con la conversación.

JINETE: ¿No son aquéllas las luces de Granada?

AMARGO: No sé. El mundo es muy grande.

JINETE: Y muy solo.

AMARGO: Como que está deshabitado.

JINETE: Tú lo estás diciendo.

AMARGO: ¡Me da una desesperanza! ¡Ay yayayay!

JINETE: Porque si llegas allí, ¿qué haces?

AMARGO: ¿Qué hago?

JINETE: Y si te estás en tu sitio, ¿para qué quieres estar?

AMARGO: What a beautiful thing!

RIDER: Who could deny that?

(*The night becomes as thick as hundred-year-old wine. The fat serpent of the South opens its eyes to the pre-dawn, and within the sleepers there is an infinite desire to hurl themselves off the balcony into the perverse magic of perfume and distances.*)

AMARGO: It seems that we've lost our way.

RIDER (*stopping the horse*): Have we?

AMARGO: While we were talking.

RIDER: Aren't those the lights of Granada?

AMARGO: I don't know. The world's such a big place.

RIDER: And so very lonely.

AMARGO: Inasmuch as it's uninhabited.

RIDER: You've said it.

AMARGO: It makes me lose hope. Ay yayayay!

RIDER: Because if you get there, what'll you do?

AMARGO: What'll I do?

RIDER: And if you were where you belong, why do you want to get there?

AMARGO: ¿Para qúe?

JINETE: Yo monto este caballo y vendo cuchillos, pero si no
lo hiciera, ¿qué pasaría?

AMARGO: ¿Qué pasaría?

(Pausa.)

JINETE: Estamos llegando a Granada.

AMARGO: ¿Es posible?

JINETE: Mira cómo relumbran los miradores.

AMARGO: Sí, ciertamente.

JINETE: Ahora no te negarás a montar conmigo.

AMARGO: Espera un poco.

JINETE: ¡Vamos, sube! Sube de prisa. Es necesario llegar antes
de que amanezca...Y toma este cuchillo. ¡Te lo regalo!

AMARGO: ¡Ay yayayay!

(El Jinete ayuda al Amargo. Los dos emprenden
el camino de Granada. La sierra del fondo se
cubre de cicutas y de ortigas.)

AMARGO: Why?

RIDER: I ride all around on this horse selling knives, but if I didn't, what would happen?

AMARGO: What would happen?

(Pause.)

RIDER: We're getting close to Granada.

AMARGO: Is that possible?

RIDER: Look how the balcony windows are glittering.

AMARGO: Yes, that's true.

RIDER: Now you won't refuse to ride with me.

AMARGO: Wait a while.

RIDER: Come on, jump on! Climb up fast. We've got to get there before day breaks... And take this knife. I'll give it to you!

AMARGO: Ay yayayay!

(The rider helps Amargo up. The two of them set off towards Granada. The sierra in the background becomes covered, with cactus and nettles.)

CANCIÓN DE LA MADRE DEL AMARGO

Lo llevan puesto en mi sábana
mis adelfas y mi palma.

Día veintisiete de agosto
con un cuchillito de oro.

La cruz. ¡Y vamos andando!
Era moreno y amargo.

Vecinas, dadme una jarra
de azófar con limonada.

La cruz. No llorad ninguna.
El Amargo está en la luna.

9 de julio, 1925

SONG OF AMARGO'S MOTHER

They carry him placed upon my sheet,
upon my oleander and my palm leaves.

The twenty-seventh day of August,
with a tiny little knife of gold.

The cross. And so much for that!
He was so dark and so very bitter.

Neighbor ladies, bring me a brass
pitcher filled full of lemonade.

The cross. Don't anybody weep.
For Amargo is now in the moon.

July 9, 1925

TRANSLATOR'S NOTES

Page 41. "Archers," line 3.
Lorca means "open to the sea." The Guadalquivir is navigable all the way up to Sevilla.

Page 47. "Procession," final line.
Durandarte was originally the name of Roland's sword; later, a character in legends of Spanish literature. Here Lorca appears to be referring to *Don Quixote*, Part II, Chapter XXIII, where Durandarte's story is recounted. Durandarte asked his friend, Montesinos, to cut out his heart with a dagger and take it to Lady Belerma. ". . . a furious Orlando" is an allusion to Lodovico Ariosto's famous poem *Orlando Furioso*.

Page 77. "Portrait of Silverio Franconetti"
Franconetti (1825-1893) was the most important singer of the 19th century. His father was Italian and his mother was from Morón de la Frontera. His cabaret, Café Silverio, became the focal point of deep song during those years.

Page 79. "Juan Breva"
Juan Breva (1835-1915), whose real name was Antonio Ortega, became the first commercial artist of flamenco. Breva was the greatest singer of *malagueñas* of his time. His fame was such that he even sang at the Royal Palace. He died in poverty — after having thrown away a fortune — in his native town of Vélez-Málaga.

Page 81. "Flamenco Cabaret," line 4.
Dolores "La Parrala" was one of the great interpreters of the *siguiriya*.

Page 89. "Malagueña"
"Malagueña" is not properly part of deep song, but rather belongs to the *fandango* family. *Malagueña* also means "woman of Málaga," and Lorca plays with the double meaning.

Page 93.   "Dance," line 1.
           This is Bizet's Carmen, but now she is an old woman.

Page 99.   "Castanet"
           Crótalo has two meanings: castanet and rattlesnake.

Page 101. "Prickly Pear," line 4.
           The prickly pear plant looks like a multi-armed jai alai
           player.

CITY LIGHTS PUBLICATIONS

Angulo de, Jaime. INDIANS IN OVERALLS
Angulo de, G. & J. de Angulo. JAIME IN TAOS
Artaud, Antonin. ARTAUD ANTHOLOGY
Bataille, Georges. EROTISM: Death and Sensuality
Bataille, Georges. THE IMPOSSIBLE
Bataille, Georges. STORY OF THE EYE
Bataille, Georges. THE TEARS OF EROS
Baudelaire, Charles. TWENTY PROSE POEMS
Baudelaire, Charles. INTIMATE JOURNALS
Bowles, Paul. A HUNDRED CAMELS IN THE COURTYARD
Broughton, James. MAKING LIGHT OF IT
Brown, Rebecca. THE TERRIBLE GIRLS
Bukowski, Charles. THE MOST BEAUTIFUL WOMAN IN TOWN
Bukowski, Charles. NOTES OF A DIRTY OLD MAN
Bukowski, Charles. TALES OF ORDINARY MADNESS
Burroughs, William S. THE BURROUGHS FILE
Burroughs, William S. THE YAGE LETTERS
Cassady, Neal. THE FIRST THIRD
Choukri, Mohamed. FOR BREAD ALONE
CITY LIGHTS REVIEW #1: Politics and Poetry issue
CITY LIGHTS REVIEW #2: AIDS & the Arts forum
CITY LIGHTS REVIEW #3: Media and Propaganda issue
CITY LIGHTS REVIEW #4: Literature / Politics / Ecology
Cocteau, Jean. THE WHITE BOOK (LE LIVRE BLANC)
Codrescu, Andrei, ed. EXQUISITE CORPSE READER
Cornford, Adam. ANIMATIONS
Corso, Gregory. GASOLINE
Daumal, Réne. THE POWERS OF THE WORD
David-Neel, Alexandra. SECRET ORAL TEACHINGS IN TIBETAN BUDDHIST SECTS
Deleuze, Gilles. SPINOZA: Practical Philosophy
Dick, Leslie. WITHOUT FALLING
di Prima, Diane. PIECES OF A SONG: Selected Poems
H. D. (Hilda Doolittle). NOTES ON THOUGHT & VISION
Ducornet, Rikki. ENTERING FIRE
Duras, Marguerite. DURAS BY DURAS
Eidus, Janice. VITO LOVES GERALDINE
Eberhardt, Isabelle. THE OBLIVION SEEKERS
Ferlinghetti, Lawrence. PICTURES OF THE GONE WORLD
Ferlinghetti, Lawrence. SEVEN DAYS IN NICARAGUA LIBRE
Finley, Karen. SHOCK TREATMENT
Ford, Charles Henri. OUT OF THE LABYRINTH: Selected Poems
Franzen, Cola, transl. POEMS OF ARAB ANDALUSIA
García Lorca, Federico. BARBAROUS NIGHTS: Legends & Plays
García Lorca, Federico. ODE TO WALT WHITMAN & OTHER POEMS
García Lorca, Federico. POEM OF THE DEEP SONG
Ginsberg, Allen. HOWL & OTHER POEMS
Ginsberg, Allen. KADDISH & OTHER POEMS
Ginsberg, Allen. REALITY SANDWICHES
Ginsberg, Allen. PLANET NEWS
Ginsberg, Allen. THE FALL OF AMERICA
Ginsberg, Allen. MIND BREATHS
Ginsberg, Allen. PLUTONIAN ODE

Goethe, J. W. von. TALES FOR TRANSFORMATION
Hayton-Keeva, Sally, ed. VALIANT WOMEN IN WAR AND EXILE
Herron, Don. THE DASHIELL HAMMETT TOUR: A Guidebook
Herron, Don. THE LITERARY WORLD OF SAN FRANCISCO
Higman, Perry, tr. LOVE POEMS FROM SPAIN AND SPANISH AMERICA
Jaffe, Harold. EROS: Anti-Eros
Jenkins, Edith. AGAINST A FIELD SINISTER
Kerouac, Jack. BOOK OF DREAMS
Kerouac, Jack. POEMS ALL SIZES
Kerouac, Jack. SCATTERED POEMS
Lacarrière, Jacques. THE GNOSTICS
La Duke, Betty. COMPANERAS: Women, Art & Social Change in Latin America
La Loca. ADVENTURES ON THE ISLE OF ADOLESCENCE
Lamantia, Philip. MEADOWLARK WEST
Lamantia, Philip. BECOMING VISIBLE
Laughlin, James. SELECTED POEMS: 1935-1985
Le Brun, Annie. SADE: On the Brink of the Abyss
Lowry, Malcolm. SELECTED POEMS
Marcelin, Philippe-Thoby. THE BEAST OF THE HAITIAN HILLS
Masereel, Frans. PASSIONATE JOURNEY
Mayakovsky, Vladimir. LISTEN! EARLY POEMS
Mrabet, Mohammed. THE BOY WHO SET THE FIRE
Mrabet, Mohammed. THE LEMON
Mrabet, Mohammed. LOVE WITH A FEW HAIRS
Mrabet, Mohammed. M'HASHISH
Murguia, A. & B. Paschke, eds. VOLCAN: Poems from Central America
Paschke, B. & D. Volpendesta, eds. CLAMOR OF INNOCENCE
Pessoa, Fernando. ALWAYS ASTONISHED
Peters, Nancy J., ed. WAR AFTER WAR (City Lights Review #5)
Pasolini, Pier Paolo. ROMAN POEMS
Poe, Edgar Allan. THE UNKNOWN POE
Porta, Antonio. KISSES FROM ANOTHER DREAM
Purdy, James. THE CANDLES OF YOUR EYES
Purdy, James. IN A SHALLOW GRAVE
Purdy, James. GARMENTS THE LIVING WEAR
Prévert, Jacques. PAROLES
Rachlin, Nahid. VEILS: SHORT STORIES
Rey-Rosa, Rodrigo. THE BEGGAR'S KNIFE
Rigaud, Milo. SECRETS OF VOODOO
Saadawi El, Nawal. MEMOIRS OF A WOMAN DOCTOR
Sawyer-Lauçanno, Christopher, transl. THE DESTRUCTION OF THE JAGUAR
Sclauzero, Mariarosa. MARLENE
Serge, Victor. RESISTANCE
Shepard, Sam. MOTEL CHRONICLES
Shepard, Sam. FOOL FOR LOVE & THE SAD LAMENT OF PECOS BILL
Smith, Michael. IT A COME
Snyder, Gary. THE OLD WAYS
Solnit, Rebecca. SECRET EXHIBITION: Six California Artists of the Cold War Era
Sussler, Betsy, ed. BOMB: INTERVIEWS
Takahashi, Mutsuo. SLEEPING SINNING FALLING
Turyn, Anne, ed. TOP TOP STORIES
Tutuola, Amos. FEATHER WOMAN OF THE JUNGLE
Tutuola, Amos. SIMBI & THE SATYR OF THE DARK JUNGLE
Valaoritis, Nanos. MY AFTERLIFE GUARANTEED
Wilson, Colin. POETRY AND MYSTICISM